WHOOO! GRINS AND GOOSEBUMPS

Lightly Spooky, Funny Friendly Tales for Brave Young Readers (Ages 5-8)

VOL-1

AF517171

Rachel Wintergreen

ISBN: 9789334460513

Author: Rachel Wintergreen

Contact: storyline@svakrta.com

Website: www.svakrta.com

svakrta
STORYLINE

Introduction

Welcome, brave little readers!

Are you ready for a spooky but not too scary adventure? Inside this book, you'll discover eight ghostly tales filled with giggles, mystery, and just the right amount of chills! Each story comes with its own special illustration to bring the magic to life.

From friendly ghosts to mischievous spirits, magical pumpkins to enchanted broomsticks, every tale is packed with Halloween fun and surprises.

But don't worry... these ghosts aren't here to give you nightmares! They might rattle doors, float through walls, or play silly tricks, but deep down, they're just looking for a little fun (or maybe even a new friend... like you!).

So grab a cozy blanket, turn on your favorite nightlight, and get ready to peek into a world of friendly frights, magical mysteries, and playful hauntings!

Are you ready?

Then let's begin... if you dare!

TABLE OF CONTENTS

THREE WHITE GHOSTS AND THE MISSING PUMPKIN

Three friendly ghosts lived in a cheerful old barn in Willow Hollow, right next to the biggest pumpkin patch in town.

Pip was the littlest ghost, round and bouncy like a fluffy cloud. Mama Ghost wore a beautiful, flowing scarf that sparkled in the moonlight. Papa Ghost was tall and gentle, with a curly beard that wiggled when he laughed.

All summer long, the ghost family took care of a special pumpkin. They watered it every day, sang happy songs to it, and watched it grow bigger and rounder!

"Look how orange it is!" Pip said, floating in happy circles. "It's the most beautiful pumpkin in the whole world!"

Mama Ghost clapped her hands. "Tomorrow is Halloween, and everyone will see our wonderful pumpkin!"

Papa Ghost's whiskers twitched with excitement. "This

will be the best Halloween ever!"

The three ghosts floated back to their barn that night, dreaming of all the trick-or-treaters who would admire their beautiful pumpkin.

But the next morning, when Pip rushed outside to check on it, he froze.

"MAMA! PAPA! Come quick!" Pip cried.

Mama Ghost and Papa Ghost hurried over.

Their beautiful pumpkin was gone!

"Where did it go?" Pip's voice trembled.

Papa Ghost rubbed his curly beard thoughtfully. "Pumpkins don't just roll away by themselves."

"Wait! Look at this!" Mama Ghost pointed to the ground.

A trail of colorful candy wrappers led away from where their pumpkin had been sitting.

"Someone took our pumpkin and dropped candy along the way!" Mama Ghost said, adjusting her sparkly scarf. "Let's follow the trail!"

"Ghost family to the rescue!" Papa Ghost cheered.

The three ghosts followed the candy trail through the pumpkin patch, past the corn maze, and into Whispering Woods. The trees were old and crooked, with branches that looked like reaching fingers. Golden leaves drifted down around them like confetti.

Pip floated close to his parents. "The woods look a little scary," he whispered.

"Don't worry, little one," Mama Ghost said softly. "We're brave ghosts, and we're together."

"That's right!" Papa Ghost added. "Ghosts never give up!"

Soon, they heard voices ahead, laughing and chattering loudly.

When the ghosts peeked around a big oak tree, they gasped.

A group of mischievous goblins was dancing around a large cooking pot! The goblins had pointy hats and big grins, and they were tossing candy into the air like confetti.

And right next to the pot sat their prize pumpkin!

"Oh no!" Pip whispered. "They're going to make pumpkin soup!"

"We have to save our pumpkin!" Mama Ghost said. "But how?"

Papa Ghost grinned and wiggled his eyebrows. "With some friendly ghost magic!"

The three ghosts huddled together to make a plan.

"Here's what we'll do," Papa Ghost whispered. "Pip, you hide behind that big tree and make your best ghost sounds. Mama, you'll use your beautiful scarf to blow out their fire, very gently! And I'll appear and ask them nicely to give back our pumpkin!"

Pip took a deep breath. "I can do it! Brave ghosts don't give up!"

Pip floated behind the biggest tree. “Ooooooh!” he called softly.

The goblins stopped dancing. “What was that?” one goblin asked, his pointy ears twitching.

Then Mama Ghost floated above the pot and waved her sparkly scarf. Whoosh! A gentle breeze put out the fire.

“Hey! Who put out our fire?” another goblin yelped, looking around nervously.

That’s when Papa Ghost appeared, floating high and proud, his curly beard glowing in the dappled sunlight. “Hello there, goblins!” he said in his friendliest voice. “I think you have something that belongs to us!”

The goblins looked up and gasped. “A ghost! A real ghost!”

“Don’t be scared!” Papa Ghost said with a warm smile. “We’re friendly ghosts. But that pumpkin is ours. We’ve been taking care of it all summer long.”

The goblins looked at the pumpkin, then back at the ghost family.

The biggest goblin stepped forward, looking embarrassed. “We’re sorry, Mr. Ghost. We didn’t know it belonged to anyone. It looked like the most beautiful pumpkin we’d ever seen.”

“We wanted to make pumpkin soup for our Halloween party,” a little goblin added sadly. “But we should have asked first.”

Pip floated out from behind the tree. "You could come to OUR Halloween party instead! We always have lots of yummy pumpkin treats!"

The goblins' eyes lit up. "Really? You'd invite us?"

"Of course!" Mama Ghost said, her scarf sparkling happily. "The more friends, the merrier!"

The goblins cheered and carefully helped the ghost family carry their pumpkin back home.

That evening, as the first trick-or-treaters arrived in Willow Hollow, the ghost family's barn glowed with warm, welcoming light.

They carved their beautiful pumpkin with the biggest smile anyone had ever seen. It sat on the porch, greeting everyone who passed by.

The goblins brought candy and cookies to share. Everyone played ghost tag and told funny stories until the moon rose high in the sky.

"This IS the best Halloween ever!" Pip giggled, dancing with his new goblin friends.

"And do you know why?" Mama Ghost asked, her scarf shimmering in the moonlight.

"Because we made new friends!" Papa Ghost said, his whiskers twitching happily.

"And because we chose kindness instead of scariness!" Pip added cheerfully.

As the night grew late, the three white ghosts watched their perfect pumpkin glow in the darkness. They knew this Halloween would always be special, not just because they saved their pumpkin, but because they turned pumpkin thieves into pumpkin friends.

THE LITTLE WITCH'S BROOM

Luna was the tiniest witch in Willow Hollow, and tomorrow was Halloween! She could hardly wait.

"Finally!" she sang, spinning around her cozy cabin. "Tomorrow, I get to fly with the other witches!"

Luna hugged her special broomstick. It was just her size, with bristles that sparkled like stars.

"I've been practicing every day," Luna told Whiskers, her black cat. "Tomorrow I'll fly over the rooftops for the very first time!"

Whiskers yawned and stretched. "Just make sure your broom behaves."

Luna smiled. "It will be perfect!"

She swept the floor one last time. "Tomorrow, we fly!"

As she placed her broom in the corner, suddenly...

WHOOSH!

The broom shot across the room like a rocket!

"Whoa!" Luna gasped.

The broom wiggled and swayed in the air, then... "ACHOO!"

It sneezed! The broom knocked over spell books and spun in wild circles before crashing into a stack of potion bottles.

Whiskers stared with wide eyes. "Did your broom just sneeze?"

Luna watched in amazement as the broom floated quietly in the air, sniffling softly.

"What's wrong, little broom?" Luna asked gently.

She heard a tiny giggle coming from inside the broomstick!

Luna's eyes went wide. "Is someone in there?"

A small voice whispered, "Oops."

Luna tapped the broom handle carefully. "Hello?"

Silvery mist puffed out from the bristles. The mist swirled and sparkled, then transformed into the tiniest ghost Luna had ever seen! He was no bigger than a teacup, with twinkling eyes and a shy smile.

"A ghost!" Luna exclaimed. "There's a ghost in my broom!"

The little ghost floated nervously. "Hi. I'm Boo. I'm really, really sorry."

Whiskers' fur stood straight up. "That explains the sneezing!"

"I didn't mean to cause trouble!" Boo said, wringing his tiny ghostly hands.

Luna tilted her head curiously. "How did you get in there?"

Boo glowed pink with embarrassment. "I was playing hide-and-seek with my ghost friends in the woods. Your broom looked like the perfect hiding spot!"

"So you hid inside my broom?" Luna asked.

"Yes! But then it started moving, and I got tangled in the magic bristles! Now I can't get out!"

Luna put her hands on her hips. "That's why my broom has been acting so silly!"

"I'm so sorry," Boo said, his glow dimming sadly.

Luna's expression softened. The little ghost looked so miserable. "Don't worry, Boo. But I really need my broom to work tomorrow. It's my first time flying with the other witches."

Boo's eyes filled with ghostly tears. "Oh no! I've ruined your special night!"

"You haven't ruined anything," Luna said kindly. "We just need to get you unstuck."

Luna held her broom carefully. "Okay, Boo, try floating out."

Boo pushed and wiggled with all his might. "I'm trying! But I'm really stuck!"

Luna thought for a moment, tapping her chin. Then she smiled.

"Boo, what if you're not really stuck? What if you're just trying too hard?"

Boo peeked out from between the bristles. "What do you mean?"

"Ghosts float through walls and things, right? Maybe you forgot how because you're so worried and scared."

Luna sat down beside her broom. "Close your eyes, Boo. Imagine you're floating like a soft, puffy cloud."

"I'll try," Boo said quietly.

"Whiskers, can you purr for us?" Luna asked.

Whiskers purred deeply, filling the room with a soothing rumble.

"Picture yourself on a warm summer breeze, Boo," Luna said gently. "You're as light as air. You can float anywhere you want to go."

Boo's tiny form began to glow brighter. "I feel it! I'm getting floaty again!"

"That's it!" Luna encouraged. "Now drift out, nice and easy, like you're made of moonlight."

Slowly, like morning mist lifting from a pond, Boo floated out from the bristles.

"It's working!" Boo whispered in wonder.

With a gentle whoosh, Boo floated completely free and twirled happily in the air.

"I'm out! I'm free!" he cheered.

Luna tested her broom, giving it a little shake. It worked perfectly!

"My broom is back to normal!" she said happily.

Boo spun joyfully. "Thank you, Luna! You're the kindest

witch ever!"

Luna smiled warmly. "I'm just glad you're free, Boo."

Boo floated closer, looking hopeful. "Luna? Could I fly with you tomorrow night? I promise I'll stay OUTSIDE the broom this time!"

Luna's face lit up. "Of course! Having a ghost friend beside me would make it even more special!"

Boo glowed so brightly he lit up the whole room. "This will be the best Halloween ever!"

Whiskers stretched lazily. "Just no more sneezing, please."

The next night, the full moon rose over Willow Hollow. Luna stood on her porch holding her trusty broom. Boo floated beside her, glowing with excitement.

"Ready?" Luna asked.

"I've never been more ready!" Boo said.

Luna climbed onto her broom, and together they soared into the Halloween sky.

Below them, the town twinkled with jack-o'-lanterns and colorful lights. Other witches flew through the night on their broomsticks, their cloaks billowing in the wind. Luna joined them, feeling proud and happy.

"Look at all the lights!" Boo said, pointing at the glowing houses below.

Luna laughed as the wind rushed through her hair. "It's magical!"

"This is the best night ever!" Boo spun in happy circles

beside Luna's broom, leaving a trail of sparkles.
"It really is," Luna agreed, smiling at her new friend. "Especially with you here!"
As they flew toward the bright moon, Boo giggled. "You know what, Luna?"
"What?"
"Next time I play hide-and-seek, I'm definitely picking a tree!"
They laughed together as they soared across the Halloween sky, the little witch and her ghost friend having the most wonderful adventure of their lives.

GHOST WHO WANTED A HUG

Tommy stood in his new bedroom, surrounded by towers of moving boxes. The big old house on Maple Street was very different from their small apartment in the city.

"This place is really old," Tommy said, opening the creaky closet door.

His younger sister Emily peeked through the doorway. "It's kind of spooky! I bet it's haunted."

Tommy rolled his eyes. "Emily, there's no such thing as ghosts."

Suddenly, a soft, sad sigh floated through the room.

Tommy froze. "Did you hear that?"

Before Emily could answer, something shimmery appeared near the window.

It was a ghost! Small and round, with big, sad eyes and tiny, misty hands. The ghost floated above Tommy's bed and sighed again, even more sadly.

"GHOST!" Emily squealed and ran down the hall.

But Tommy didn't run. He just stood there, staring. The ghost didn't look scary at all. He looked... lonely.

Tommy stepped forward carefully. "Um... hello?"

The ghost's eyes lit up with hope. "Oh! You can see me?"

Tommy nodded slowly. "Yes, I can."

The ghost clapped his misty hands together. "Wonderful! I'm Wisp, and I've been waiting so long for someone like you!"

Tommy tilted his head curiously. "Waiting for what?"

Wisp floated closer, glowing with excitement. "For someone to give me a HUG!"

Tommy blinked in surprise. "A hug?"

Wisp nodded eagerly. "I don't like scaring people like other ghosts do. I just want one friendly hug. But every time I try..." He reached toward Tommy's arm, and his misty hand passed straight through. "I float right through everything!"

Tommy felt his heart ache. "You mean you've never been hugged? Ever?"

Wisp sank lower in the air. "Never. Not once in fifty years."

"That's really sad," Tommy said softly.

Tommy took a deep breath. "Well, let's try!"

He opened his arms wide and stepped forward... WHOOSH!

He walked right through Wisp! A cold, tingly feeling swept through Tommy's whole body, making him shiver.

Wisp looked even sadder. “See? It never works.”

But Tommy wasn’t giving up that easily. “Don’t worry, Wisp. We just need to figure out the right way to do it.”

Wisp floated a bit higher. “You really think there’s a way?”

“I know there is!” Tommy said confidently. “Halloween is coming soon, and that’s the most magical night of the year. We’ll find a way to give you a real hug!”

Wisp’s eyes sparkled with hope. “Do you really mean it?”

“I promise!” Tommy said.

Over the next few days, Tommy tried everything he could think of.

First, he wrapped a blanket around Wisp while trying to hug him. But the ghost floated right through the soft fabric like it wasn’t even there.

Next, Tommy had Wisp float into a big, fluffy pillow while he hugged it from the other side. But Wisp drifted through the pillow like morning mist.

Then Tommy tried holding his favorite stuffed bear while Wisp floated beside it. “Maybe you can feel the hug through Mr. Cuddles?”

But Wisp’s ghostly hands slipped right through the soft fur.

Wisp’s shoulders slumped. “It’s no use, Tommy. I guess ghosts just can’t be hugged.”

Tommy refused to give up. "Not yet, Wisp. I made you a promise."

Then Tommy noticed something important. Every time Wisp tried to hug something, Tommy felt that cold, tingly sensation. And when Tommy wore his thick winter coat during one experiment, the tingling felt much stronger and lasted longer.

"Wisp!" Tommy said excitedly. "I think I've figured it out!"

On Halloween night, while his family got ready for trick-or-treating, Tommy had something more important to do.

He put on his puffiest winter coat. Then he wrapped his softest scarf around his neck three times. He added his warmest hat, pulled on his fluffiest mittens, and even stuffed an extra sweater underneath everything.

Emily watched from the doorway, puzzled. "Why are you dressed for a snowstorm? It's not even cold outside."

Tommy smiled mysteriously. "You'll see."

He waddled up to his room like a penguin, so bundled up he could barely move his arms.

Wisp was floating by the window, looking sadder than ever.

"Okay, Wisp!" Tommy called. "I figured it out!"

Wisp turned around. "Figured what out?"

"How to give you the best ghost hug ever!"

Tommy stood in the middle of the room, looking like

the fluffiest, roundest snowman anyone had ever seen. All the thick layers made him twice his normal size. He spread his puffy arms wide.

"Try hugging me now!"

Wisp hesitated, then slowly floated forward. He wrapped his misty arms around Tommy and...

This time something magical happened!

Tommy felt the cold, tingly sensation, but the thick, fluffy layers caught and held some of Wisp's ghostly form. Tommy could actually feel the soft pressure of ghostly arms around him!

And for the first time in fifty years, Wisp felt the warmth and coziness of a real hug.

"I can feel it!" Wisp whispered in wonder. "I can actually feel the hug!"

Tommy squeezed gently, careful not to squeeze too hard, and Wisp let out a happy gasp.

"I told you we'd figure it out!" Tommy said with a huge grin.

"This is the happiest moment of my entire ghostly life!" Wisp laughed, glowing so brightly he lit up the whole room.

Just then, Emily peeked around the doorframe. "Tommy, Mom says it's time for trick-or–" She stopped and stared, her mouth falling open. "Are you hugging the ghost?"

Tommy nodded, still holding Wisp gently. "Yep!"

Emily's eyes grew wide with wonder instead of fear. "That's so cool! Can I try too?"

Wisp's eyes sparkled with joy. "Two hugs in one night? This is incredible!"

Emily raced to her room and quickly bundled up in her thick winter coat, a puffy vest, and her warmest scarf. She spread her arms wide.

When she hugged Wisp, she giggled at the tingly, cold feeling. "This is the coolest hug ever!"

Wisp spun in happy circles, glowing brighter than the jack-o'-lanterns outside. "Best Halloween EVER!"

From that night on, Wisp was the happiest ghost on Maple Street. He had finally found what every ghost and every person needs most: friends who care enough to find a way to show their love.

And whenever Tommy or Emily needed a special, tingly, ghost hug, Wisp was always there, ready to share the warmth of friendship.

THE GIGGLE GHOSTS OF HOLLOW STREET

Every night around nine o'clock, the people in Willowbrook heard a very strange sound. Soft giggles would start along Hollow Street, getting louder and louder until the whole neighborhood echoed with mysterious laughter.

At first, adults thought it was just the wind. But night after night, the giggles grew stronger, bouncing from house to house, rattling windows, and making dogs howl.

"It's coming from the old Hartwell house," Mrs. Peterson whispered to her neighbor. "I saw glowing lights in the windows!"

"I heard the giggles turn into wild cackling!" Mr. Lopez said, shivering.

Soon, everyone was talking about the spooky house at the end of Hollow Street. Kids were rushed inside before dark, and even the mailman started running past the old, creaky building.

But Tim and Tilly, eight-year-old twins who lived just three houses away, weren't scared at all. They were curious.

One Tuesday night, as the giggles began again, Tim pressed his nose against their bedroom window.

"Tilly, come look!" he whispered excitedly. "I can see sparkly lights dancing inside!"

Tilly jumped over and peered out. "Those don't look like scary ghost lights. They look... happy!"

Tim nodded thoughtfully. "But ghosts are supposed to say 'BOO!' and rattle chains, not laugh."

"Well, these ones are definitely laughing," Tilly said, grabbing her shoes. "Let's find out why!"

The twins grabbed their flashlights and snuck outside. Hollow Street looked different at night, with long shadows stretching across the sidewalk. The old Hartwell house stood ahead, its windows glowing with soft, golden light.

The laughter got louder as they got closer. It sounded like kids having the best time ever!

Tim swallowed nervously. "What if they don't want visitors?"

Tilly grinned. "Then we'll just make them laugh even harder!"

When they reached the house, the front door creaked open by itself, as if it had been waiting for them. The twins stepped into a dusty hallway, their flashlight beams dancing across faded wallpaper.

Giggle, giggle, giggle!

The sound came from the living room. Tim and Tilly crept forward and peeked around the corner.

They gasped.

Three ghost children were having the biggest tickle fight ever! They were bright and see-through, but they looked like regular kids, except they were laughing so hard they could barely breathe.

A boy ghost with messy hair and a crooked grin spotted them first. He floated over, still giggling.

"Oh! Hi there! Welcome to our Giggle House!" he said between laughs.

Tim and Tilly exchanged surprised glances. These ghosts weren't scary at all!

"I'm Pip!" the messy-haired ghost said. "That's Willa!" He pointed to a girl with curly hair who was floating upside down, laughing. "And that's Gus!" A round, cheerful boy waved while doing somersaults in the air.

"We heard you laughing every night," Tilly said, stepping forward bravely. "The whole neighborhood can hear you! But... why are you laughing so much?"

Pip tried to look serious but burst into giggles. "We can't help it! We have a laughing curse!"

"A laughing curse?" Tim asked.

Willa nodded, wiping ghostly tears from her eyes.

"Three months ago, we were playing hide-and-seek in this house and found an old magic book in the attic."

"When we opened it," Gus added between giggles, "a huge cloud of sparkly dust covered us! Now we laugh at everything, even when we don't want to!"

"We've tried everything to stop!" Pip said, then immediately started laughing again.

Tim scratched his head thoughtfully. "Have you tried... laughing quieter?"

The three ghosts stopped and stared at him.

"Quieter?" Willa repeated.

"Yeah!" Tilly said excitedly. "You can still have fun and laugh, but maybe practice doing it softly so you don't wake up the whole town!"

Hope sparkled in the ghosts' eyes.

"Do you think that could work?" Gus asked.

"Let's try!" Tim said. "Tilly, tell them a joke."

Tilly leaned close to Pip. "Why don't skeletons fight each other?"

Pip bit his ghostly lip, trying not to laugh. His cheeks puffed up like balloons.

"Because they don't have the guts!" Tilly finished with a grin.

Pip couldn't help but laugh, but this time he covered his mouth with both hands. Instead of echoing through the house, it came out as a soft "hee-hee-hee" that sounded like wind chimes.

"It worked!" Tim cheered quietly.

The ghosts practiced their quiet laughs. Willa learned to cup her giggles in her hands like she was catching butterflies. Gus discovered he could make cute little snorts if he laughed into a pillow.

For a whole week, Tim and Tilly returned every night to help their new friends practice. They whispered jokes, played quiet games, and taught the ghosts how to have fun without driving the neighborhood crazy.

The ghosts were eager students. By the seventh night, they could laugh so softly that even mice couldn't hear them.

"You did it!" Tim said proudly.

"We couldn't have done it without you two," Pip said, giving them ghostly high-fives that felt like cool butterflies on their hands.

"You're the best friends ever!" Willa added with a grateful smile.

As Tim and Tilly walked home that night, Hollow Street was finally peaceful. The neighbors could sleep soundly, and the ghosts could still play together happily.

From that night on, the giggles stopped bothering anyone. But on very quiet nights, if you listened carefully, you might still hear the sweetest, softest giggles floating on the wind–the sound of three happy ghosts who learned that having fun doesn't always have to be loud.

THE SECRET PASSENGERS IN A CAR

Kinsley pressed her nose against the dusty window of Grandpa's old green car. It had been sitting in the shed for ten years, covered in cobwebs and dust.

"It looks like a big green box with wheels," she giggled, drawing a smiley face in the dirt.

Dad opened the creaky door. "Smells like old books in here."

The leather seats were cracked but still soft. Kinsley bounced into the passenger seat. "Does it even work anymore?"

"Let's find out!" Dad turned the key.

The car grumbled and coughed, then suddenly roared to life. "VROOM!"

"It's alive!" Kinsley cheered as they backed out of the shed.

At first, everything seemed normal. The sun was

shining, birds were singing, and Kinsley was excited for their drive.

But then something felt strange.

Even though it was a warm day, the car felt oddly chilly inside. Not scary cold, just peculiar.

Click! The radio turned on by itself.

A scratchy voice came through the speakers. "Ooh, we're going on a trip!"

Kinsley's eyes went wide. "Dad! Did you hear that?"

Dad laughed. "Old cars make funny sounds sometimes."

Swish, swish! The windshield wipers started moving, even though the sky was perfectly clear.

Dad scratched his head. "Okay, that IS weird."

Then the strangest thing happened. The seat beside Kinsley suddenly sank down, like someone invisible had just sat there.

"Hee-hee-hee!" a small voice giggled right next to her ear.

"Dad, STOP!" Kinsley squeaked.

Dad pulled over under a big shade tree. "What's wrong?"

Kinsley slowly reached her hand toward the empty seat.

Poke.

Her finger touched something cool and soft, like a cloud.

"HEE-HEE! That tickles!" a voice laughed.

Suddenly, four see-through figures appeared in the car!

A tall ghost father with a fluffy beard and twinkling

eyes. A ghost mother with a warm smile and sparkly pearl earrings. A little ghost girl doing flips in the air. And a ghost boy about Kinsley's age, grinning right beside her!

"Don't be scared!" the ghost boy said. "I'm Pip! You're sitting in my favorite spot!"

Dad's jaw dropped. "G-g-ghosts?!"

The ghost mother laughed gently. "We're the Carlington family! This car has been our home since it was abandoned. We made it cozy."

The little ghost girl, Luna, twirled in the air. "But now that it's moving again, we can't get out!"

Kinsley's eyes sparkled with excitement. "So YOU'RE the ones making the radio turn on and the wipers move?"

Pip nodded proudly. "We like playing tricks! We were so bored just sitting still for all those years."

For the next hour, the ghost family had the best time with Kinsley and Dad.

Luna floated out the window and waved at people passing by. Some waved back nervously. Others just stared with their mouths hanging open!

Pip made silly faces at drivers in other cars, making them laugh without knowing why.

Ghost Dad tried singing along to the radio but kept getting the words hilariously wrong, making everyone giggle.

"This is the most fun ever!" Kinsley laughed. She tried to high-five Pip, but her hand went right through his. They both giggled even harder.

"I like you, Kinsley!" Pip said. "You're not scared of us at all!"

As they drove past the old stone bridge near town, Ghost Dad stroked his fluffy beard thoughtfully. "You know, family, we've been in this car for a very long time. Maybe it's time we found a proper home."

Ghost Mom nodded. "Somewhere peaceful where we can rest."

Pip and Luna's faces fell. "But we like it here! And we like Kinsley!"

Dad stopped the car by the river, next to a beautiful old oak tree. Its branches hung low with Spanish moss, and the water sparkled like diamonds in the sunlight.

"How about here?" Dad suggested softly.

Ghost Dad floated over to look at the tree. "This feels just right. Peaceful and pretty."

Ghost Mom tried to hug Kinsley, but her arms floated right through. "Thank you for the wonderful ride, dear. You made us feel so welcome."

Pip and Luna gave Kinsley see-through high-fives. "We'll miss you!"

Kinsley felt happy and sad all mixed together. "I'll miss you too!"

Pip winked. "Maybe we'll visit you next Halloween!"

The four ghosts spun around like leaves caught in the wind, then disappeared with a soft whoosh into the old oak tree.

As they drove home, the car felt different. Warmer. Quieter. Normal.

But also a little bit empty.

Dad shook his head in wonder. "That was the strangest road trip ever."

Kinsley smiled, looking back at the oak tree growing smaller in the distance. "It was the BEST. I really hope we see them again."

And somewhere in the old oak tree by the river, four friendly ghosts settled into their new home, remembering the brave, kind girl who wasn't afraid to be their friend.

THE MONSTER FEARED BY THE DARKNESS

Wobble was a unique little monster who lived in the magical town of Whimsy Hollow, where pumpkins got rounder and witches made the best hot chocolate. He was blue and fluffy like a cloud, with sparkling eyes and a round, squishy belly that jiggled when he laughed. But Wobble had a secret that made him different from other monsters.

He was scared of the dark.

Every evening as the sun set behind the purple hills, Wobble would peek out from his cozy cave and start to worry. "Oh no," he would whisper, wrapping his soft tail around himself. "Soon it will be dark, and the scary shadows will dance on my walls!"

When darkness fell, strange shapes would twist and move across Wobble's cave walls. They looked like monsters with big teeth, dragons with flapping wings, or skeletons dancing around. Even though they were only shadows, they still made him shake with fear.

One fall evening, as Wobble watched the sun go down, a bright little light bounced toward him.

"Boo!" called out a happy voice.

Wobble jumped so high that he tumbled backward into a pile of leaves. Crackle, snap, rattle!

A small, bright ghost floating in the air giggled. "Gotcha! I'm sorry, Wobble! I'm just practicing for Halloween!"

Wobble stood up and brushed the colorful leaves off his fur. "Glimmer! You scared me!"

Glimmer was Wobble's best friend, a tiny ghost who shone like a warm, friendly star. She loved Halloween and was always practicing her "boos" and flying tricks.

"I need to get ready for the Halloween Glow Parade!"

"Glimmer," she said, spinning in a circle. "It's only three days away!"

Wobble's ears drooped. "I wish I could enjoy Halloween like you do."

Glimmer floated closer. "Are you still scared of the dark, buddy?"

Wobble nodded sadly. "I know it's silly. I'm supposed to be a monster, but I'm scared of scary things!"

Glimmer's glow grew warmer. "That's not silly at all! Everybody is scared of something. I'm terrified of vacuum cleaners!"

Wobble couldn't help but giggle. "Really?"

"Really! They're so loud and whooshy!" Glimmer

shivered. "But wait, I have an idea! What if I stay with you tonight? I could light up your cave!"

Wobble's eyes sparkled with hope. "You would do that for me?"

"Of course! That's what best friends are for!" Glimmer beamed. "I'm the brightest ghost in all of Whimsy Hollow!"

That night, Wobble felt much better as he got ready for bed. Glimmer floated nearby, giving off a soft glow like the perfect nightlight.

"This is wonderful," Wobble yawned, curling up in his warm blankets. "No scary shadows tonight!"

But then something strange happened.

Flash, flash, flash...

Glimmer's light started to flicker and dance. Suddenly, her glow cast wild, moving shapes on the cave walls! One shadow looked like a giant spider with wriggling legs. Another looked like a three-headed dragon breathing fire. And one even looked like a skeleton doing the chicken dance!

Wobble's fur stood straight up. "AHHH!" He dove under his blanket. "Glimmer! Your light is making them even bigger!"

Glimmer gasped. "Oh no! I'm so sorry! I made things worse!"

Wobble peeked out from under his blanket. His best friend's glow was dimming because she looked so sad.

“its okay, Glimmer,” Wobble said gently. “You were trying to help. Maybe we just need to figure out how to make your light less... shadow monster-y.”

Glimmer brightened a little. “But how?”

Wobble thought hard, tapping his fuzzy chin with his paw. Suddenly, his tail started wagging excitedly.

“I’ve got it! The Halloween Glow Parade!”

Glimmer tilted her head. “What about it?”

“Every year, the whole town lights up with happy, beautiful lights! Maybe they can show us how to make light fun instead of scary!”

Glimmer’s glow grew brighter. “That’s brilliant! Let’s go!”

They hurried into town just as the parade was starting. Wobble couldn’t believe his eyes. The streets sparkled with friendly jack-o’-lanterns wearing big smiles. Glowing pumpkins floated through the air like orange balloons. Fireflies twinkled like tiny stars, and paper lanterns shaped like friendly bats and cats swayed gently in the breeze.

“Look, Glimmer!” Wobble pointed excitedly. “See how they use light to make everything magical and happy instead of scary?”

Glimmer watched carefully. “I think I understand! I need to shape my light into something wonderful instead of just glowing randomly!”

“Can you try?” Wobble asked hopefully.

Glimmer concentrated hard, and her light began to shimmer and sparkle.

Sparkle, whirl, POOF!

Her glow transformed into a cheerful pumpkin!

"You did it!" Wobble cheered.

Glimmer spun around, and her light changed again, this time into a playful cat chasing its tail. Then it became a friendly ghost wearing a party hat!

The parade watchers stopped and clapped. "How amazing!" they cheered.

Wobble laughed and bounced around. "This is wonderful! I'm not scared at all!"

Glimmer glowed with pride. "And guess what? You're not afraid of my light anymore!"

Wobble realized she was right. "You're absolutely right! I'm not scared!"

Back in Wobble's cave that night, Glimmer floated around, creating beautiful, happy shapes with her light. Dancing butterflies, cheerful suns, and twinkling stars filled the cave with warmth and wonder.

Wobble snuggled into his bed, feeling safe and cozy. "Glimmer, you're the most amazing friend a monster could ask for."

"And you're the bravest monster I know," Glimmer said softly. "You faced your fear and found a way to make it better."

Wobble yawned sleepily. "I think I like the dark now...

as long as it has your special glow."

From that night on, Wobble wasn't afraid of the dark anymore. He learned that scary things can become beautiful when we look at them in a new way.

When Halloween finally arrived, Wobble happily joined the Glow Parade, walking proudly beside his best friend Glimmer as she put on the most magical light show Whimsy Hollow had ever seen.

THE HAUNTED LIBRARY'S SECRET KEEPER

Eleanor loved going to the library on Saturday evenings. The old wooden floors creaked a friendly greeting when she walked on them, and the air smelled like old books and adventures waiting to happen. She always curled up in the same cozy corner with a stack of picture books as the sun went down.

But lately, strange things had been happening.

Eleanor heard whispers, but they weren't coming from people. They were coming from the books! Pages would turn by themselves. Words would sometimes float through the air like tiny, glowing butterflies.

"I must be imagining things," Eleanor whispered to herself.

But one evening, as she reached for her favorite book about a friendly dragon, she heard a soft giggle from the shelf beside her.

"Hello?" a gentle voice asked. "Is someone there?"

THUMP!

A book tumbled to the floor right beside her feet. Eleanor jumped, her heart pounding like a drum. Carefully, slowly, she picked up the book and turned it over.

A tiny ghostly figure about the size of her thumb peeked out from behind it. His wispy hair glowed softly, his blue eyes sparkled, and his coat shimmered like moonlight.

"Oh my goodness!" he said in the sweetest voice. "You can see me!"

Eleanor's eyes went wide. "You're... you're a ghost!"

The little ghost floated up to eye level. "My name is Pip. I'm the library's Secret Keeper." He looked terribly worried. "And I really need your help!"

Eleanor sat down cross-legged to see Pip better. "What kind of help?"

Pip wrung his tiny hands nervously. "I take care of special stories, ones that people have almost forgotten. I hide them in safe places so they won't be lost forever." His voice grew quieter. "But I've lost three of them!"

"Lost them?" Eleanor gasped.

"They were here yesterday!" Pip said, floating back and forth anxiously. "If we don't find them by midnight tonight, Halloween night, they'll disappear forever. Stories lose their magic when nobody remembers them anymore."

Eleanor's heart sank. Stories disappearing forever? That was the saddest thing she could imagine. "I'll help you find them!"

Pip glowed brighter with hope. "Really? You'd do that for me?"

"Of course!" Eleanor said warmly. "I love stories more than anything. We can't let them disappear!"

And so their treasure hunt began.

Pip led Eleanor to the fairy tale section first. "I think I hid The Singing Teapot somewhere around here," he said thoughtfully.

Eleanor searched everywhere. She peeked under bookends shaped like owls and behind thick encyclopedias. Finally, way at the bottom of the lowest shelf, she found a tiny golden scroll tied with a purple ribbon.

"That's it!" Pip cheered, doing a happy loop-de-loop in the air.

When Eleanor touched the scroll, it sparkled like fairy dust. Then it burst into twinkling lights that danced around the shelves before settling into an old fairy tale book.

"The library remembers it now," Pip said with relief. "It's safe!"

"That was magical!" Eleanor whispered. "Where's the next one?"

They searched the astronomy section next, looking for

The Case of the Missing Moon. Pip remembered hiding it in a small atlas. Eleanor found it tucked between two heavy books and carefully opened it. The words inside glowed silver and swirled like a gentle snowstorm before landing safely in a book of bedtime stories.

"One more to go!" Pip said, though his face looked more worried now. "The Story of Halloween Magic is the last one, and it's the most important. Every year, it's what keeps the library's special magic alive."

Eleanor understood why this one mattered so much. Without it, Pip might disappear, and the wonderful, magical feeling of the library might be gone forever.

"Where do you think it could be?" she asked.

Pip scrunched up his face in concentration. Then his eyes flew wide open. "The old fireplace! I wanted to keep it extra safe and warm!"

They hurried to the big stone fireplace that hadn't been used in many years. Eleanor knelt down and carefully reached inside. She felt around behind the dusty iron grate until her fingers touched something small and rectangular.

She pulled out a tiny book. The words "Halloween Magic" were written across it in letters that seemed to shimmer and change colors.

"Got it!" Eleanor whispered excitedly.

Pip gasped with joy. "You found it! You really found it!"

As Eleanor held the little book, it glowed with the

most beautiful light she'd ever seen. Purple and orange sparkles swirled through the library like playful spirits having a celebration. The light touched every book at once, making the whole library feel alive with happiness.

"Thank you, Eleanor," Pip said, shining so brightly he looked like a little star. "You saved the stories, and you saved the library's magic too."

Eleanor felt warm and proud inside. "Will I see you again?"

Pip winked with one twinkling blue eye. "Every Saturday evening, if you'd like. There are always more stories that need keeping safe."

As Eleanor prepared to leave, she heard the books around her whispering "thank you" in voices as soft as butterfly wings.

She smiled up at Pip. "I'll see you next week!"

From that night on, Eleanor wasn't just visiting the library anymore. She was working with Pip to rescue forgotten stories and keep the magic alive, one adventure at a time.

THE FRIENDLY FEAR AT 13 OAK LANE

Jasper had a problem. He was supposed to be a scary ghost, but he was terrible at it.

Every morning, Jasper floated to the dusty attic mirror in the old house at 13 Oak Lane and practiced making his scariest face. He opened his eyes wide, puffed out his cheeks, and took the biggest, deepest breath he could.

"BOO!" he yelled.

But it didn't sound scary at all. Instead, it came out as a tiny squeak that sounded more like a baby mouse saying hello.

Jasper sighed, making the cobwebs flutter. "That's not scary at all."

Jasper had lived in the creaky old house at 13 Oak Lane for as long as he could remember. According to every ghost handbook, when new families moved in, you were supposed to scare them away. That was Ghost

Rule Number One.

But Jasper had never scared anyone. Not even once.

His last family had called him "charming." The family before that had said he was "adorable." One little girl had even tried to hug him!

"This time will be different," Jasper told himself as he watched a bright yellow moving truck pull into the driveway. "I'm going to be the scariest ghost ever!"

Out of the truck came a boy with curly red hair and shoes shaped like dinosaurs. He carried a backpack covered in rocket ship patches and looked about seven years old.

"Perfect," Jasper whispered to himself. "Kids are supposed to be easy to scare."

That night, when the house was quiet and moonlight streamed through the windows, Jasper gathered all his courage. He floated down the hallway toward the boy's room and practiced his "BOO" one more time.

The boy, whose name was Leo according to what Jasper had heard his mom call him, was reading a book about space explorers in bed.

Jasper took the deepest ghost breath of his life.

"BOO!" he shouted, appearing right beside Leo's bed.

Leo looked up from his book. "Oh! Hi there!"

Jasper blinked in surprise. "Hi? You're supposed to scream!"

"Why?" Leo asked, setting down his book. "Are you a

ghost?"

"Of course I'm a ghost!" Jasper huffed. "I live here! I'm supposed to haunt this house!"

Leo hopped out of bed, looking excited. "Wow, a real ghost! That's so cool! Can you rattle chains?"

Jasper's shoulders slumped. "Well... no."

"Can you walk through walls?"

"I get stuck sometimes," Jasper admitted quietly.

"What about making spooky 'Wooooo' sounds?"

Jasper tried his best. "Wooooo–" But it came out as a soft "Whoooo," like an owl asking a polite question.

Leo giggled. "You sound like my baby sister when she's sleepy!"

Jasper felt himself growing dimmer and more transparent. "I'm the worst ghost ever. I'm just not scary enough!"

Leo sat down on his bed and looked at Jasper thoughtfully. "Maybe you don't have to be scary. Maybe you're a different kind of ghost."

"Different how?" Jasper asked, floating a bit closer.

"Well," Leo said, "what if you were a helpful ghost instead of a scary one?"

Jasper had never thought of that before. "But... but Ghost Rule Number One says–"

"Forget the rules!" Leo interrupted cheerfully. "You could be the first friendly ghost ever! Why scare people when you could help them instead?"

Jasper felt a tiny spark of hope. "What kind of help?"

Leo grinned. "Well, I lose my socks all the time. Could you help me find them?"

Jasper concentrated hard and made Leo's missing sock float out from under the bed. Leo's eyes grew huge with amazement.

"That was awesome!" Leo cheered. "What else can you do?"

For the first time in his ghostly life, Jasper felt happy instead of sad. He made Leo's pencils dance across the desk, organized Leo's books by color on the shelf, and even floated a glass of water from the kitchen upstairs without spilling a single drop.

"You're not a scary ghost," Leo said with a big smile. "You're an amazing ghost! A helpful ghost! A ghost friend!"

Jasper glowed brighter than he ever had before. "Really?"

"Really! Being helpful is way better than being scary."

From that night on, Jasper stopped trying to scare people and became Leo's best friend and secret helper. When Leo couldn't find his homework, Jasper would float it to him from under a pile of papers. When Leo felt sad, Jasper would make him laugh by drawing funny faces in the dust that danced in the sunlight. And when Leo had trouble sleeping, Jasper would hum gentle songs that sounded like summer wind through the trees.

Soon, Leo's whole family noticed that their house felt special. Nobody knew why missing socks would appear right when they were needed, why lost keys were always found in just the right place, or why the house always felt warm and cozy.

But Leo knew. Every night before bed, he would whisper "Thank you, Jasper" to his invisible friend.

And Jasper would whisper back, "Thank you for helping me discover what kind of ghost I'm meant to be."

Jasper learned that being kind was so much better than being scary. Leo learned that the best friends aren't always the ones you expect to find.

And they both learned that being different isn't something to fix. It's something to celebrate.

OTHER BOOKS BY AUTHOR

(AVAILABLE & COMING SOON)

1) Yes! You Are an Amazing Girl (6-12)
2) Yes! You Are an Amazing Black Girl (6-12)
3) Yes! You Are an Amazing Black Boy (6-12)
4) Yes! You Are an Amazing Boy (6-12)
5) Yes! Brave, Bold, Blonde, That's Me (6-12)
6) Yes! We Are Amazing Girls Around the World
7) Pony Tales: Stories for Young Riders (7-12)

8) Fun Bedtime Stories for Younger Kids (4-6)

9) Fun Bedtime Stories for Older Kids (7-10)

10) Campfire Stories for Kids (8-12)

11) Lights Off: Spooky Stories for Kids(8-12)

12) Whooo! Grins and Goosebump

Vol. 1: Spooky Stories for Kids (5-8)

13) Whooo! Giggles and Shivers

Vol. 2: More Spooky Stories for Kids (5-8)

14) Short Stories for Seniors

15) A Little Elf Tobin: A Fantasy Adventure

9 789334 460513

Printed at Repro India Ltd.